This Book
is otherwise
provided to you
as-is

by Jonathan Ball

Martian Embassy Media
PO Box 70043 Kenaston PO
Winnipeg, MB, Canada R3P 0X6
www.martianembassymedia.com

**Welcome To The World of Free Plain Vanilla
Electronic Texts**
**Books Readable By Both Humans and By
Computers, Since 1971**

— Project Gutenberg edition of Edgar Allan Poe's
The Fall of the House of Usher

CHAPTER ONE
BELSHAZZAR (H. RIDER HAGGARD)

At that moment the moon that had been half hidden by a cloud, shone out fully. End of this Project Gutenberg of Australia Book *Belshazzar* by H.

How soon men forget the voices of those they thought fair enough to hold close not a sunrise ago! Taking the lamp we crept up the stairs, I going first with my sword ready. While we hesitated, hiding ourselves as best we could, the tidings came, whence I could not see. She sprang from her chair, saying, Follow me!

Never will I fall living into the jaws of yonder dog. Here in Vermont the affair was not so picturesque as it might have been on the Western prairies.

I thought that you had gone with the other, I said. Hart and may be reprinted only when these Books are free of all fees. While we hesitated, hiding ourselves as best we could, the tidings came, whence I could not see.

Shall we not earnestly cooperate to bring in the new day? At that moment the moon that had been half hidden by a cloud, shone out fully.

I am he whose young daughter you wronged and murdered long ago. In those good days women really had a chance. Despite these efforts, the Projects Books and any medium they may be on may contain Defects.

He took me by the hand, he led me away, and I remember no more till I found myself in this place. Some of that glittering mob were overthrown and trampled, among them my mother. I caught it up and threw it over Myra's gorgeous bridal robe, drawing the hood over her head.

It is not to be found in superficial politics or in mere economic blunders.

CHAPTER TWO

GONE WITH THE WIND
(MARGARET MITCHELL)

Scarlett, we must get him hidden before the folks come back from the swamp. There was something vital and earthy and coarse about him that appealed to her.

Besides, there was some pleasure in shouting at people and knowing they were afraid. She slipped it into place with a hand that did not shake.

Rhett was wrong when he said men fought wars for money. The Yankees can't force it down our throats if we won't have it. The ladies knew the gentlemen were lying and the gentlemen knew the ladies knew they were lying.

Fontaine had said another child would cost her her life. She wondered why, knowing that even a month before she could never have done the deed.

Don't dare try to help me either or I'll carry you

upstairs myself. There was a God after all, and He did provide, even if He did take very odd ways of providing. A Yankee, a Yankee with a long pistol on his hip!

I think you are hateful to talk to Baby and me like this! Suppose it should gangrene like the soldiers' wounds and she should die, far away from a doctor? Before he could even fumble at his belt, she pulled the trigger.

It's over and done with and I'd have been a ninny not to kill him. Yes, Tara was worth fighting for, and she accepted simply and without question the fight.

Go back to bed, she threw over her shoulder. Don't dare try to help me either or I'll carry you upstairs myself.

How careless they had been of food then, what prodigal waste! Life treated women well when they had learned those lessons, said Ellen. Here was the Wilkes pride in the dust at her feet. Rolls, corn muffins, biscuits and waffles, dripping butter, all at one meal.

Scarlett bent over, caught the dead man by his boots

and tugged.

She crossed it cautiously and trudged uphill the hot half-mile to Twelve Oaks. The only time crying ever did any good was when there was a man around from whom you wished favors. It was just part of her nicey-nice way of acting which had always made Scarlett despise her. Ellen was the audience before which the blustering drama of Gerald O'Hara had been played.

No one questioned whence the horse had come. The road lay still and deserted and never a cloud of red dust proclaimed the approach of visitors. She crossed it cautiously and trudged uphill the hot half-mile to Twelve Oaks. She was not recovering as she should and Scarlett was frightened by her white weakness.

He didn't like yams, he repeated; wanted a drumstick and some rice and gravy. I'll think of it later, she said aloud, turning her eyes away.

Read it, said Melly, pointing to the letter on the floor. Oh, Scarlett, how could you have brought this on me? Scarlett cried, but the half-naked Melanie made her painful way down into the lower hall.

CHAPTER THREE

AN AMERICAN TRAGEDY
(THEODORE DREISER)

Tell me, he added curiously at this point, does your husband know of this? That's a funny request for a fellow like that to make of me.

Motherhood should hold no serious consequences for you. And yet, as he argued with himself, how could the occasion ever be more satisfactory? Indeed, as at first, his manner remained seeking and not a little sycophantic at times. I amused to such things year in and out, whatever they are.

I am only a country doctor, you know, and I hope I'm not as dreadful as you seem to think. It would be so much better if we could go at night. You seem to me to be a strong, healthy girl. I think maybe I'll take this one, anyhow, and this one, too.

Then, by degrees, for Clyde at least, there was a slight lifting of the heavy pall. Oh, I don't know what I shall do unless I find someway out of this.

But he knows that you're in trouble, doesn't he? How are things with the Griffiths Company anyhow?

Not nearly as hard as you think or as wicked as this other way. Maybe you can tell me what I want to know.

For after all, what did he know about how she felt? Tell me, he added curiously at this point, does your husband know of this? Ordinarily it was his custom to advise immediate and unconditional marriage. I amused to such things year in and out, whatever they are.

But in this instance I'm sure the situation isn't one which warrants anything like that.

CHAPTER FOUR
CONFESSIONAL (FRANK HARRIS)

My coach in mathematics and English was a young teacher, just out of college. My coach in mathematics and English was a young teacher, just out of college.

My coach in mathematics and English was a young teacher, just out of college.

My aunt and I came back home somewhere towards midnight. Copyright laws are changing all over the world. So let us see what the Catholic Church made of its governmental problem.

I opened this and the contents certainly dumfounded me. I was only a month in college when she wrote to tell me that she was in the family way. I could not speak: my tongue stuck to my dry mouth.

They held the body in a vault until I returned.

In short, the perfect liberty of which slaves dream

because they have no experience of its horrors. As I look back at it through the years I am sure now that there was no thought of sex in my mind.

The problem of love and sex is a most difficult one.

Few boys have been blessed with as happy a home as this uncle and aunt made for me. Few boys have been blessed with as happy a home as this uncle and aunt made for me. There was never a word of scandal about the whole affair. I had many girl friends, but no sweetheart. Since our marriage the thought of another woman has never entered into my head.

THIS BOOK IS OTHERWISE PROVIDED TO YOU AS-IS. That wonderful sexual energy must have a rational outlet. Few boys have been blessed with as happy a home as this uncle and aunt made for me. They held the body in a vault until I returned.

This night I was smoking a cigarette sitting in an easy chair in my room when my aunt came in again. It was ten days old before I could get to see it, as the baby was born in a hospital. Hart and may be reprinted only when these Books are free of all fees.

As between these two processes of bleeding and being bled, bleeding is the better fun. So let us see what the Catholic Church made of its governmental problem.

Leisure is the sphere of individual liberty: labor is the sphere of slavery. My sex nature suddenly awoke and could not be satisfied, it would seem. Her sex nature was pent up too, for I was later to learn that my uncle was not strong sexually. Where, then, was the offence that so exceedingly disgruntled these unhappy persons?

I was a far more brilliant scholar in college than I ever was in high school. She was a splendid mother to me, and she made an ideal wife for my uncle. The bank opened my uncle's safe-deposit box and found his will.

A sweeter, purer wife and mother never lived than my wife. I opened this and the contents certainly dumfounded me. As I got up to fourteen or so my uncle started to tell me some things a boy should know. My aunt's mother came to live with us and after a year we were quietly married.

It was ten days old before I could get to see it, as the baby was born in a hospital. The poor have been pitied for miseries which do not, unfortunately, make them unbearably miserable.

CHAPTER FIVE
SHADOWS ON THE ROCK
(WILLA CATHER)

And in France where do the swallows go in winter? It was up there that one looked, from the back door, for the first sign of spring.

Father Hector tasted his wine, inhaling it with a deep breath. I am peculiarly susceptible to the comforts of the fireside and to the charm of children. Father Hector tasted his wine, inhaling it with a deep breath. How many times, out there, I shall live over this evening again, with you and Cécile.

Oh, Pierre Charron, I am delighted at you, Pierre Charron! He was never the same man after she shut herself away.

Very clearly, Euclide, it was arranged in Heaven that I should be a missionary in a foreign land. Charron sat silent for a moment, then bent over the candle and lit his pipe, which had gone out. There was our tree, heaped over with snow, with the opening to the south still clear. I was afraid of him, for he was a hard man.

I am not clever with tools, like my brother-in-law. Auclair felt disturbed, a little frightened. Your sickness was a good chance for you, my poor fellow. And now, Cécile, said her father, shall we tell Father Hector our secret? I will put a card on the door announcing that we are closed until noon.

Auclair began to wonder whether Pierre might have had anything to drink before he came to dinner. Tomorrow I will go to Father Sébastien, and between us we will cure his distress. But he had another misery, harder to bear than his jaw. Others have their family; but to a solitary and an exile his friends are everything.

Auclair had put his glass to his lips, but set it down untasted. No man ever gave up more for Christ than Noël Chabanel; many gave all, but few had so much to give. He said it was right to punish the wicked, but I could never get used to it.

Early the next morning Father Hector was ready to start back with me. He would have made away with himself then, but he was afraid of being punished after death.

Cécile slipped her hand into Charron's, and they went out into the street. She was gracious and gentle, as always, and at her ease.

CHAPTER SIX
THE END OF A CHILDHOOD
(HENRY HANDEL RICHARDSON)

For she was the best friend I ever 'ave had, and the oldest, too. You could look through it at night to where Luce slept with Bowey. You could wear your tongue out, explaining. Bowey wouldn't let him ask other children in: I don't know if your Ma would like it. In vain he protested: When Papa died we only had bands on our sleeves.

I don't know, said Cuffy simply and truthfully. Anyhow, there it was: I started to cry, and it just jumped out. These found and one struck, the candle was recovered; but the candlestick lay in fragments. Never had Tilly seen such wide, astonished eyes.

As long as he was out in the garden it didn't bother him much. But that was all, and he didn't like it; and he simply couldn't imagine. But Uncle Jerry lived ever such a long way off; and it was two whole days before he got there. But the next minute things began buzzing round in his head like angry bees.

Awful days, that seemed as if they'd never end.

Hand-in-hand Cuffy and Lucie went back to the garden, and sat down on the wood of the wood-stack. And as Cuffy still stood fixing her, she added: It's no good looking at me like that. But I know you won't mind turning in together.

But I know you won't mind turning in together. For all of a sudden, as the last familiar landmarks went by, something funny happened to him. To begin with, Uncle Jerry was in a dreadful hurry. Or do you mean we're not going to live here any more?

Bowey wouldn't let him ask other children in: I don't know if your Ma would like it. It's your Pa you take after, both of you, more's the pity.

But your face was the one bit of you you couldn't put under water.

But even though he could manage to forget her face, he wasn't really happy. Everything looked just like it always did and yet was somehow quite different. And suddenly she turned tail and ran back to the pool. They started to watch for the coach long before it was time. When this was up to their knees, they stooped to damp napes and crowns, and sluice their arms.

But what did the old hag mean by her cheek about me? Nobody came: and gradually his face cooled off, his heart stopped thumping. Even Mamma being dead didn't seem to matter so much.

CHAPTER SEVEN
A TANGLED WEB (L. M. MONTGOMERY)

Do you think Barry would have liked it, dear? This left a sore spot in Peter's soul which envenomed still further his hatred of Donna Dark. Life had not been an empty cup for her, whatever bitter brew was mingled in it. So Peter came to the levee, but he felt a bit grim and into the house he would not go.

But Peter never made any allowances for that.

Gay never forgot the first day she and Nan had met. He had grey eagle eyes, that turned black in excitement or deep feeling. Not that it seemed to matter much to Joscelyn whether they forgave her or not.

The state of affairs was accepted as something permanent and immutable. Margaret would have been a little fluttered had she known he was thinking even this much. Of course Aunt Becky didn't like her, but then whom did Aunt Becky like? If their delicate, exotic beauty was wasted on Aunt Becky, it was not lost on Margaret.

He had had one keen greedy look at Joscelyn when he had paused a moment in the doorway. Meanwhile she took care of him and worshipped him. Nobody whom Noel loved would ever grow old and unlovely.

He always averred he could not breathe with four walls around him. She knew she could never care for any man again. Margaret's bones seemed to melt in her body as water when she thought of it. Gay Penhallow was sitting next to Margaret and was not thinking of the jug at all.

For ten years they had continued to wear weeds, though Virginia was always much weedier than Donna. If he had a vanity it was in the elaborate anchors tattooed on the back of his hands.

Her father was like that, you know, Mrs Clifford Penhallow wept. You know, his grandfather reads those horrid Ingersoll books.

He considered them far more tasty and much more in keeping with the sea than Drowned John's snake.

He had had one keen greedy look at Joscelyn when he had paused a moment in the doorway. Besides, the jug would give her a certain importance. What the divvle could have come between her and Hugh? So Peter came to the levee, but he felt a bit grim and into the house he would not go.

Every Sunday Drowned John went into the graveyard and guffawed over it. The winter before, he had had double pneumonia and everybody was sure he would die. Joscelyn had seen Hugh when he came into the room. Joscelyn had confessed she was a kleptomaniac. For one, she knew all the Penhallows rather disapproved of Noel Gibson. They were always expecting him to be killed.

If she had set her heart on that confounded jug, he wasn't going to spoil her chance. Of course Aunt Becky didn't like her, but then whom did Aunt Becky like? Aunty But had never seen anything like it.

If she had set her heart on that confounded jug, he wasn't going to spoil her chance. But they never missed attending any clan gathering.

CHAPTER EIGHT
APACHE DEVIL
(EDGAR RICE BURROUGHS)

They wore grave faces as they approached Geronimo. They intended to get us between them and kill us all. When a man tries to do right, people should not tell bad stories about him. The woman felt the edge of a knife against the flesh at her throat. He is ready to give up and come in and be a good Indian.

If we stand and fight them many of us will be killed. We cannot hope to win.

Make noise, gettum killed, whispered a deep voice. Crawford snatched his pistol from its holster and covered Shoz-Dijiji. General Crook addressed Geronimo almost immediately. For a half hour they watched, then Giannah-tah withdrew, silently as a shadow.

Only fools attack when they know they cannot win. Perhaps they were off their guard, but then, even Homer is charged with carelessness. I went away with my wife and children to live in peace as my own people have always lived.

If they kill Geronimo they will kill Na-chi-ta also, said Shoz-Dijiji. I have thought of that, replied Na-chi-ta.

Geronimo knows that I have no authority to do that. Did Na-chi-ta send you with this message? If you stay out I'll keep after you and kill the last one if it takes fifty years. Thus spoke Kut-le, the bravest of the renegades. He says that they are boasting about what they are going to do to Geronimo and his band.

When their brief council was concluded, Geronimo arose.

When did Shoz-Dijiji begin to fear trouble with the white-eyed men? Has Nan-tan-des-la-par-en told you to take warriors and stop the sale of fire water to the Apaches? He has told you that they are his friends. Another day, when our warriors are sober, we can fight them but not today. How may drunken men defend their families and themselves? That we would come and make camp near him this afternoon. They are planning to join forces against us.

It is senseless to fight under such circumstances. If we must be killed let us be killed in battle and not shot down from behind by drunken white-eyes.

A tree fell upon the man in such a way that he could not free himself. She's in the next tent, she whispered hastily. He is my oldest son, replied Pedro, wondering.

If not we can pick our own time and place to fight.

CHAPTER NINE

LANDTAKERS: THE STORY OF AN EPOCH (BRIAN PENTON)

Sometimes several would hiss together, like leaves shaken in the breeze.

Don't remember much about England, Gursey muttered. But Gursey withheld himself, brooding with Peters over a dark secret. The sound of an axe came down with the wind. For two hundred yards round the pens the trampling feet of the sheep had worn all the grass away.

One shop has got a glass window ten, twelve times as big as an ordinary window. McFarlane's long face which seemed to be made of rubber, stretched three inches longer.

The black yellow-bellied snake and the more poisonous brown one were everywhere. I thought we'd have some peace and quiet here. McFarlane's long face which seemed to be made of rubber, stretched three inches longer. They'll kill him, and it will be all my doing, all my doing.

McGovern's too lazy to come all this way out. When I think back I seem always on the point of discovering, but some treacherous devil blinded me. Sometimes several would hiss together, like leaves shaken in the breeze. He was afraid to touch anything, to take a step in the darkness.

Something in his voice made McFarlane glance up. One day I cheeked the boss and he ironed me up in the woolshed. But he thought, Pity I destroyed those three hundred old ewes. And all the time needles of throbbing agony thrust up into his temple.

Open your gob and I'll yank it out for you. They'd cut your throat, he suggested, laughing to drive away uneasy thoughts of his own. She pulled her horse round and tried to ride past him, but he blocked the narrow way. You could have the lambs tomorrow, he told her.

Ye ken, I couldna remain under the same roof after that. That whitish skin, them daisy feet, them little fingers. It's Peters who told you that drunken gossip.

Does t' old scut think God made man to scurry round like a pack of hounds after his strays? He picks her up like a cheeld then and carries her oot.

All be broke up into small splinters with one hit from that Jem. I was going to pay you a call as soon as I got things a bit straight here, he said. Cabell added a plate of cold potatoes, a damper, a flask of rum and a bottle of pickles to the meal.

He spurred his tired horse into a canter, seeing figures appear in the doorway. He was deprived of breath for the moment, as though by a violent blow in the stomach. Dennis has got tables and chairs you can move about in his pub.

CHAPTER TEN
CERTAIN PEOPLE (EDITH WHARTON)

There's no wireless in the desert, sir; not like London. But perhaps she had only stopped to push back a strand of hair as she passed in front of a mirror.

Copyright laws are changing all over the world. His respectful tone tempered the slight irony.

The smooth slippery floor of the hall seemed to Nora to extend away in front of her for miles. Fastidiously he wiped a trail of grease from his linen sleeve. And the minutes were slipping by, and upstairs the man she loved was lying.

Loyally, Christopher always pretended that she didn't; talked of her indulgently as poor Jenny. It was odd to have feared so defenseless an adversary.

The silence, the remoteness, the illimitable air!

I 'ope that Perrier'll turn up tomorrow, sir. He IS

interested in tree moving, isn't he? The water is sure to be boiling, because the nurses' tea is just being taken up. He sent me such an interesting collection of pamphlets about tree moving.

The man, who was young and muscular, with a lean Bedouin face, stopped and looked at him. There's no wireless in the desert, sir; not like London.

The noontide is upon us and our half waking has turned to fuller day, and we must part.

And not a single old reliable among them? She started up and pushed her way out of the train.

Christopher is so devoted to his friends. But when he's here he needs me for himself; and when he's away he needs me to watch over the others.

CHAPTER ELEVEN
THE AUTOCRACY OF MR. PARHAM
(H. G. WELLS)

It was astounding to find how superficial loyalty to the Empire had always been. Now, hard upon the heels of the naval tragedy, came the new war in the air. The military authorities arrested vigorously. The tale of these domestic casualties lengthened. What's a flag for if you're never going to wave it?

There were pogroms in Hungary and Roumania. Blow upon blow rained upon him after that opening day of calamity.

A heart of steel, echoed the Lord Paramount. Arrest the agitators and shoot a few of them, if you don't like firing on crowds. He was now almost full size again and confident and abrupt in his pre-war style.

Blow upon blow rained upon him after that opening day of calamity.

He was declining to be a bulldog altogether. He had seen his war east of the Vistula and Danube and with its main field in Asia. He tried to steel his heart to that disappointment, but the pain was there. I tell you, it's not only street-corner boys and Bolshie agitators who are going against the wall.

This killing of honest and straightforward people who don't agree with you! If you question them they go: the ages of faith knew that. I will fight to the end, said the Lord Paramount. His role had been the godlike suppression of rebellious disorders. I'd have brought them here for you to see if I'd thought they would have weighed with you.

The simple beliefs, incredible as fact but absolutely true for the soul. But humbug does not pretend to be something unless it pays to do so. Perhaps they did not think, but just went on with their job in its new aspect. An inner necessity obliged him to read it aloud, distasteful though it was in every line.

These United States have not been able to remain aloof.

CHAPTER TWELVE
THE COMMON READER: SECOND SERIES (VIRGINIA WOOLF)

The French Revolution had passed over his head without disordering a single hair. As he said himself, he was not by nature a recluse. He lost and won and vowed never to play again, and then he did play again.

Such for many years had been the routine of Cowper's life with Mary Unwin. He would discourse upon Homer and Virgil and perhaps attempt a few translations himself. Cowper would be forced to choose between them.

The French Revolution had passed over his head without disordering a single hair. Cowper's curse had come true for both of them. At once Cowper wrote to her kindly but firmly admonishing her of the folly of her ways.

He had no advantage of birth, and but little of fortune. He lost and won and vowed never to play again, and then he did play again. Yet perhaps it was an event partly because it revived some half-forgotten but still pungent memories.

People objected to his presence in the dining-room of the hotel. He was, moreover, the most careful of artists. She made the days seem full of movement and laughter. He was, moreover, the most careful of artists.

Clearly, therefore, De Quincey as an autobiographer labours under great defects.

They had lived side by side for many years in methodical monotony. As he said himself, he was not by nature a recluse. The burden of the prophet was not laid upon him.

CHAPTER THIRTEEN

THE MIDDLE PARTS OF FORTUNE: SOMME AND ANCRE (FREDERIC MANNING)

We want to keep that, until we can have a quiet beano on our own. He refused to walk up to A Company's billets with Bourne, who went with Martlow eventually. Serves you all bloody well right, cried an exultant chorus.

I knew you couldn't 'elp not 'avin a proper at; but you shouldn't 'ave said anything. Keeperin's a funny sort o' game; but my dad's a good ol' sport. Is that clear to your somewhat atrophied intellect?

I expect 'e's for the electric chair all right.

Here, open it quick; and let's all have a tot, and then put the rest away in your pack. We're all right as we are, the three on us, aren't we? You've got a cushy job with the sigs until you go 'ome, an' you don't want to go askin' for trouble. She's a nice woman; and she had all the trouble.

Colonel Bardon passed, like some impersonal force,

and the tension relaxed. Why the 'ell can't they do the thing quick, instead of puttin' it all on us? Did you hear what he said about the regimental? I don't mind bein' on the mat, if its wo'th it, said Martlow reflectively.

Don't you ever forget that 'e does all the bloody work. Madame had all the trouble; you might put a bit extra in the kitty for her just before we go. I suppose they only sent the bread to fill up the box, but it will come in useful with the chicken.

He went back to his billet for his pack, and then with Shem and Martlow set off on their new career. Why the 'ell can't they do the thing quick, instead of puttin' it all on us? There's no sense in our going, unless we are going over the top with the company.

I know you don't want to leave the company. You don't want to sit there showin' the 'ole bloody world all you've got. Apparently they don't know what they're going to do with us when we go into the line.

That Lance-Corporal Miller is my prisoner, an' I'm responsible for 'im. Why don't they send us back to the company for the attack?

CHAPTER FOURTEEN
30,000 ON THE HOOF (ZANE GREY)

His bellow brought Mitchell around just in time to meet a blow like that from a battering-ram.

That red-headed sergeant got red in the face. On the sunny sidewalk he waited the Government man's pleasure. He found Mitchell's office empty and vacated.

Lieutenant Caddell witnessed your signature.

Mitchell has been playing high jinks among the Flagg girls. Morning came, cold and drab, with wind moaning in the trees presaging winter. And I swear I think more of you for your innocence.

There was a telegram on the floor of his room just inside the door. At length he was forced to leave the building without having seen a single army official. I saw you take the money and sign the receipt, and I witnessed it. He buttoned his wallet inside his vest and resolved to have his eyes about him.

A neat pile of cut newspaper and tinfoil pieces spread out over the table. He might be low-down enough to work on Barbara with this cattle deal. It was long after dark when Huett, after getting lost twice, found his hotel.

Humph, grunted the Senator, and taking the card, he resorted to the telephone. He wired to Kansas City for an offer, and then hunted up Doyle. But before he averted his eyes, Logan caught a fleeting glimpse of an extraordinarily steely flash. The war went on, now of secondary interest to Huett.

Next day he received an answer to his telegram. He might be low-down enough to work on Barbara with this cattle deal. It always was wonderful to see Abe get set and aim.

Lee gave the number to be thirty-one thousand and sixth odd. Mitchell called after him: Your family will suffer for your pig-headedness! Holbert and Doyle were the first to make a move. Thus far in his life of vicissitudes he had not yet been beaten down by adversity.

You're either drunk or crazy, replied Mitchell,

sharply. He had three sons at the front, and that was doing more than his share towards whipping Germany.

CHAPTER FIFTEEN
O LOST: A STORY OF THE BURIED LIFE (THOMAS WOLFE)

The German government has imperialistic designs upon the whole of the world.

The elder soda-jerker, scowling, drew a sopping rag across a puddle of slop upon the marble slab. Give me a dope, said Willie Goff to the grinning jerker, a dope and lime.

I wouldn't be caught dead with the little pimps. They've dug them up later and found them turned over on their faces.

You may, said George Graves, reeling with laughter, but I don't. You can't tell, George Graves said gloomily. Yes, said George Graves more hopefully, and that stuff they use would kill you anyway. Handsome would curl up and die if he ever took a chew.

Horse Hines came out quickly on long flapping legs,

and opened the doors behind. He arrived on hands and knees, but under his own power. His broad dark face was wreathed in Persian smiles.

Coker closed the door and sat down at his untidy desk. An Episcopalian, when I go, said George Graves with irreverent laughter. It is looking to the day when it shall have all mankind under the yoke of Krupp and Kultur. Eugene quickly drew a dirty handkerchief from the old man's pocket, and thrust it into his hands.

I'd like another statement from you before you go, Mr. The world shook with the stamp of marching men.

Ben loped along, scowling, by Wood's pharmacy. George Graves and Eugene entered Wood's pharmacy and stood up to the counter. And, with rough but affectionate camaraderie, he would pause from time to time to say: Old Male! George Graves and Eugene continued up the hill.

I'd like another statement from you before you go, Mr. Because he could not leave them, save by the inch, they moved off several yards to the curb.

Horse Hines came out quickly on long flapping legs, and opened the doors behind. What's it going to be like, ten years from now? The people who laid the town out didn't have any vision.

CHAPTER SIXTEEN
THE DOOR WITH SEVEN LOCKS
(EDGAR WALLACE)

For a moment he had been paralysed by the fantastic sight, but now the spell was broken. The girl will be rich now, though, said Sneed.

The room was empty when they turned on the lights. Lord Selford will tell us that in the morning, said Dick briskly and looked at his watch. For, strange though it may sound, Dick's heart was hottest against Stalletti for this one crime.

The strain, he admitted, was beginning to tell upon him. The seventh lock snicked back, and as he pulled the heavy door swung slowly open. If you don't derive profits, no royalty is due. Let us go inside, said Havelock; we shall disturb them with our voices.

He pulled out the contents and put them on the floor. It was the paper Dick had found in the box. Dick gazed, spellbound, as the giant crouched and reached down a hand. Wait in the hall, Sneed, and don't so much as cough until I shout.

If you don't derive profits, no royalty is due. To the truth of the foregoing we, the undersigned, set our hands.

If I'd only killed him that night I found what they'd done! I might have been able to give you a great deal of assistance. For that crime alone, Havelock, you shall go to the scaffold! Then he passed down the stairs and into the hall, where Sneed was waiting for him. The man with the candle was feeling the panelling.

It also tells you how you may distribute copies of this Book if you want to. It also tells you how you may distribute copies of this Book if you want to. Evidently Mr Havelock was cogitating this news.

He waited ten minutes and then, noiselessly unlocking the door, he stepped out into the corridor. I knew before that that he was deeply involved in this case. First a warning, musical; then the hour, irrevocable. Its effect upon the group was extraordinary.

He killed him because Stalletti told him to. We agreed eventually that it should take the shape which now appears. The detective, who had not explored the wood, wondered where the chase would end.

CHAPTER SEVENTEEN
TWELVE STORIES
(STEEN STEENSEN BLICHER)

As the moors become larger and more frequent, the churches and villages are fewer and farther apart. Alas, it was not as in former days and gave but little satisfaction!

Surely it can't be more difficult than Latin. Just as we were opposite Graakjaer, a wild boar rushed out and made straight for the squire. He fired, and hit it all right, but did not kill it, and the boar went for him. It was with a lighter heart that I ploughed these wild waves two years ago.

It seems to bring a greeting from my home. My gun hangs there dirty and rusty, and I don't care to bother about cleaning it. She was silent, and pretended not to hear, though he spoke loudly enough. My conscience condemns me and makes a coward of me.

So now I am a servant in the squire's family. Alas, it was not as in former days and gave but little satisfaction!

You found death, would that I had found it, too! She didn't even see me when I passed through the room.

My conscience condemns me and makes a coward of me. A little later I came down to fetch tow for the bullets.

I took one of the reins in either hand, and thus had both my arms round her. I felt as if I were flying through space with her, and we were at Fussingöe before I knew it. The master patted him a long time and looked sadly at him. Let me reflect on the rapture I felt; it is only now that I seem to awaken as from an intoxication.

Now it's quiet as a monastery; the new master doesn't care about the chase. A cold wind blew in our faces and carried her sweet breath back to me; I drank it in like wine.

After all, Jens has a kind heart, but he is wild and flighty. Now it doesn't please her to speak, he said, but when we get home, she'll set her mouth going. Fire, Martin, or the boar will ride to hell with me, he screamed.

So I shall not move again before I am carried to my

last home. She blushed, looked down at her plate, and smiled, but I grew cold as ice through my whole body. But the most curious thing is that I have almost gotten over my lovesickness.

Now the house looks to me as if it had been newly whitewashed and embellished. A fear, a loathing, as when one suddenly sees a viper, seized me. And where is the end of my miserable life?

A little later I came down to fetch tow for the bullets. I too shall try my luck and eat my bread among strangers. He will not live, that I could plainly see.

CHAPTER EIGHTEEN
A PRINCE OF THE CAPTIVITY
(JOHN BUCHAN)

Well, let's get round the library fire, for it's going to freeze. Joe can hand you out the rough stuff and you only like him the better for it. He peered inside the fishing-bag which lay on the moss.

There was one on the river to-day, said Adam, a man called Utlaw from Birkpool. Maybe, but we've been too long here for me to take a bagman's view of property. Also my feeling about the comedy of it all.

From the chimneys spires of amethyst smoke rose into the still evening.

My car's parked at the Town Hall and I've mislaid my chauffeur. But there's no booty, only an overdraft at the bank. The world could do with more like him to-day.

Jacqueline Armine had a voice so musical and soothing that whatever she said sounded delicious. Oh,

I don't say that Sniffy is much of a thinker, but he's a human being, which is something. You've often said you wanted to make a domestic pet of a Labour leader.

Adam's base was his chambers in the Temple. Besides, the present Parliament was hopeless, and to be a member of it would only compromise him. Is there any fellow in that show who can pull things straight? I had hopes of Kit Stannix, but I'm afraid the machine is too strong for him.

The Christian Scientists with large soft hands and a good bedside manner. If I hadn't a game leg I could dance a jig.

An hour later the sun came out and Adam sat himself on a ridge of dry moss to eat his sandwiches. No, I'm not much of a fisherman, though I love it. He's a big swell in his Union, and I'm told as red as they make 'em.

CHAPTER NINETEEN
NINETEEN EIGHTY-FOUR
(GEORGE ORWELL)

Since he was arrested he had not been fed. You don't think the Party would arrest an innocent man, do you?

All past oligarchies have fallen from power either because they ossified or because they grew soft. Just say who it is and I'll tell you anything you want.

Julia woke at the sound, stretched herself luxuriously, and got out of bed. How small, thought Winston, how small it always was! Or perhaps it was merely the shaking of his own. It should have been easy, but he always lost count at some point or another.

Which side is winning is a matter of complete indifference to them.

The man's face, already very pale, turned a colour Winston would not have believed possible. That's the one you ought to be taking, not me! His mouth had swollen into a shapeless cherry-coloured mass with a black hole in the middle of it. Heard what I was saying, and nipped off to the patrols the very next day.

The man had actually flung himself on his knees on the floor, with his hand clasped together. The demeanour of the black-uniformed men suddenly became more subdued. More prisoners came and went, mysteriously.

He was not certain that he would use the razor blade even if he got the chance. In this place, he knew instinctively, the lights would never be turned out. I suppose we may as well say good-bye, she said. It was starting, it was starting at last! It was starting, it was starting at last!

Unthinkable to disobey the iron voice from the wall. It was my little daughter, said Parsons with a sort of doleful pride. In Oldspeak it is called, quite frankly, reality control.

There was a snap as though a catch had been turned back, and a crash of breaking glass. He sat as still as he could on the narrow bench, with his hands crossed on his knee. Nor, in the circumstances, did it strike him as very important or interesting. How many times he had been beaten, how long the beatings had continued, he could not remember.

He was not certain that he would use the razor blade even if he got the chance. But there was the razor blade; they would send the razor blade if they could.

He was in a high-ceilinged windowless cell with walls of glittering white porcelain. One thing alone mattered; to keep still, to keep still and not give them an excuse to hit you! Something crashed on to the bed behind Winston's back.

CHAPTER TWENTY
GOOD-BYE TO WESTERN CULTURE
(NORMAN DOUGLAS)

Would that China could civilize the West!

Up to the present they have not had much chance of displaying this quality as public functionaries. Love of principles and lack of sympathy are not to be distinguished in their results. He will die for his principles; no harm in that. Love of principles and lack of sympathy are not to be distinguished in their results.

This is reflected in a series of nineteen articles by M. One hopes, in every case, that they are being well trimmed by some friend or by their servants.

They believe in expediency as opposed to abstract principles. At present, God being good, we are up a tree. Would that China could civilize the West!

English people poke fun at Hanuman's exploit. They are penned as closely as sardines, but in less regular order. There he died at a patriarchal age, after writing memoirs which are a veritable godsend. There are four volumes of them; forty would not be too much.

Your Frenchman, like many brave people, has a pronounced streak of masochism in his nature. It is to be hoped that these articles will appear in book form like those of M. Far from it, though their equipment might not always be adequate for modern needs.

What trouble it has cost, hitherto, to obtain the repeal of some hopelessly senile exactment! Here, then, is a second and different touchstone of civilization.

She is, on the other hand, too unnatural to inspire either reverence or fear or loathing. A man who calls women congenitally unprincipled may look out for squalls. We have seen the process at work in England. Whoever wishes to abolish syphilis should begin by abolishing hypocrisy.

They realize that every act of man is unique of its kind.

CHAPTER TWENTY-ONE
THE HOUSE OF THE ARROW
(A. E. W. MASON)

Hanaud exhorted her with a friendly smile and Ann joined the others in the dark hall. Somehow she stood upright, swaying as she stood. Frobisher led the way along the passage until the foot of another flight of steps was reached.

They did not quite close, and between them a golden strip of light showed like a wand.

We, Girardot shall make the laughter at the Assize Court! Hanaud stole over the boards and laid his ear to the panel. The man who had closed the door moved to his side as he dismounted. Hanaud had given credit to him for an astuteness which he did not possess.

Tomorrow you will tell me why you went to Madame Le Vay's ball. Hanaud's voice called to them from within the room. To the surprise of those three a second shadow flitted to her side.

It is exact to the minute, he declared with a little accent of triumph. Yes, Hanaud explained, as the door closed upon the Commissaire. It is exact to the minute, he declared with a little accent of triumph. Hanaud exhorted her with a friendly smile and Ann joined the others in the dark hall.

She was cold, as though she had slept long in her arm-chair. Tomorrow you will tell me why you went to Madame Le Vay's ball. There Madame Raviart came to live whilst she waited to be set free. Thank you, Monsieur, she replied with a wan effort at a smile. But there was more romance in that, to be sure.

He drew his coat closely about it and for a fraction of a second flashed his torchlight on the dial. You sent me to Madame Le Vay's — on purpose. He turned the key and drew the door towards him. The two figures at the window flitted back across the gallery.

Hanaud closed the door upon them and returned to the clock. A moan of pain broke from her lips, and with that consciousness returned to her. Ann shivered at the memories of that night, but she answered quietly: Yes.

Jim Frobisher was driven to the little Louis Quinze clock upon the marquetry cabinet. It remained low and quiet, but hatred crept into it, a deep, whole-hearted hatred. She sprang up now to her full height, her heels together, her arms outstretched from her sides.

What were you doing in the treasure-room yesterday evening with your watch in your hand? And you, Monsieur Frobisher, will you release that young lady, if you please!

CHAPTER TWENTY-TWO
TITANIC AND OTHER SHIPS
(CHARLES HERBERT LIGHTOLLER)

Then nobody would have had a ghost of a chance. Out of the rope we made our fishing lines. Then back with their booty to the lair, leaving no track or trace.

In the entrance to the lagoon the wreck of H. Sure enough, it was a real pool of pure clear crystal water. When the backwash came, I could feel that rope dragging through my hands, inch by inch. At the point of an albatross beak is a hook, almost exactly resembling a lion's claw.

Now in what books have I read about mirages? Peep of day next morning saw us scrambling up the cliffs aiming for the top of the island. Then back with their booty to the lair, leaving no track or trace. Then back with their booty to the lair, leaving no track or trace.

Then I further noticed that they seemed to be

actually drinking. With the result, that, I came a terrific cropper on the rocks below.

We expected all four masts to come down like a row of ninepins. Over that edge, and it would be all up for me. Or, to put his ship straight at it, and deliberately throw her away. I had good eyesight too, but perched up there I could see nothing resembling house or hut. Or else he was not as lucky as the rest of us in dodging the backwash. Arrived at the huts, the first cry from the fellows already there was, Have you found water?

So the strongest formed a sort of bodyguard, wilst we youngsters became the carriers. I could see the fellows walking ahead, but they seemed a mighty way off. From time immemorial sailing ships have what is termed Run their Easting Down. Stand clear below, was the caution, and then let go!

They had just time to slip their anchors, and run her as hard as they could for the beach. If we had not been made of cast-iron we certainly could not have stuck it. Everything on the island seemed poisonous. When the albatrosses scented the pork and the rabbits, they rose in a cloud to share a cheap meal.

One could almost describe it as a relief from the racking suspense when at last she struck.

Very likely he would be trying to sight the island to correct his position. As almost everybody was on the starb'd side of the boom, I nipped along to the port side.

I don't blame them altogether, but when, on occasions, they drew knives, then it got beyond a joke.

CHAPTER TWENTY-THREE
ARROWSMITH (SINCLAIR LEWIS)

But of course Mother would obligingly go, and leave him to conquest. In some villages in Africa, fifty per cent of the people have it, and it is invariably fatal.

Why should YOU be spared the work of memorizing your materia medica and so on and so forth? She peered up with the alert impudence of a squirrel.

The guinea pigs were in a glass jar, rigid, their hair ruffled. Davidson, how do they know ichthyol is good for erysipelas? Angus Duer glided in, demanding, Look here, old son. Young man, do you set yourself up against science?

Myron Schwab discourse on The One Way to Righteousness. He adjusted the gas light a quarter inch, and mused, Splendid! I don't seem to get along with this military discipline. He could often get through half a page of it before he bogged down in chemical formulae. Well forget most of 'em, and besides, we can always look 'em up in the book.

The first affair to which she enticed him was her big New Year's Party in January. Yes, of course, some day I guess they'll have a car every twenty minutes, he said weightily. The first affair to which she enticed him was her big New Year's Party in January.

If I can't do that and do some scientific work too, I'm no good. That summer he spent with a crew installing telephones in Montana. Martin had an excitement not free from anxiety.

He was particularly tedious in materia medica. Have they ever experimented on a whole slew of patients together, with controls? Martin had an excitement not free from anxiety. They made their own breakfasts; they dined on hash at the Pilgrim Lunch Wagon or the Dew Drop Inn.

CHAPTER TWENTY-FOUR
ANTHONY ADVERSE (HERVEY ALLEN)

Cibo pointed to the now positively decorous coachman in a clean, white jacket, and grinned. The shards of broken glass seemed to have been retrieved from his dream.

At one end of your spine is a brain and at the other end something that needs constant companionship. Since the death of the father the transactions of the firm have been in slaves.

Suppose I am successful and return with the cargo. The statue could never be put together again. It is not merely a French priest we are discussing, is it?

Tell him, Herman, he said to Meyier, or he will find out for himself. Under the window some shrub in the patio emitted a sickeningly sweet, musky scent. Listen, let us not devote more time to our Brother François.

Old Señor Gallego has recently died and his son is

in Africa. The child emerged alive and came toward him out of the chest.

Underneath the coat was a tight, white shirt with an open breast and pleated ruffles. I think I see the basis of your feeling under all this. It is modesty, you see, señor, which has kept me from speaking out.

The man dropped his handful of trailing gulf weed, squared his shoulders and looked pleased. But very shortly it will end in a tragedy for Brother François. You now hear the most profound of all human oracles speaking. What is the amount owed by Gallego and Son to the Casa da Bonnyfeather?

Mere bumboats are always told to sheer off by the officer of the deck. Adiós then, señor, at least I may wish you pleasant dreams. What do you mean, you rascal, by coming for me with rope traces?

Come, come, Toni mio, you are not going to try THAT way? He and Señor Santa María and the like had all but succeeded in diverting the revenues when I arrived. But I must insist at least on knowing the reasons why you will not answer my questions. Suddenly they drew up before the tailors.

Yes, he said, I shall accept either of your words, OF COURSE. It is not merely a French priest we are discussing, is it? Cibo and Brother François now seemed to be fighting over nothing important at all. He thought he got up and went to his chest to make sure.

The horses' heads were hanging, but all pointing down toward the new road along the edge of the gorge. Children ran up the street after it holding out their hands and screaming.

The last thing Anthony saw was the two mules trying to gallop in. The angle of incidence, he told himself, had been nicely calculated. The little catch was pulled out; therein fastened through the ring.

CHAPTER TWENTY-FIVE
THE ISLAND OF DESIRE
(ROBERT DEAN FRISBIE)

How you seduce men to your haunted shores, but only to destroy them! For a few moments Anchorage Island had been reduced in size to about five acres!

Johnny tried to help me, but the first sea that swept through the shallows nearly carried her away. Still a few smokes left in the tobacco tin! Up went Vagus' bowsprit in a wild heave, adding another ton or two of strain on the anchor. A big tot of it was taken gratefully by all hands.

The sparrow hawk is in the ground-house sleeping with the children. They are here now, and they'll have to stay until the weather moderates. Yes, Pratt agreed, and break out a dozen c-c-cans of beer.

Already half of your Anchorage Island has been swept away. Already half of your Anchorage Island has been swept away. We had a good breakfast, then we left the clearing to walk toward the lagoon beach.

A year before World War II he sailed out of England, with a partner, for the West Indies. I find that I am not writing very coherently.

He ought to know, for he comes from an island infamous for its hurricanes. Oh well, I suppose that most of us in the South Seas acquire similar characteristics. I helped him down from the beacon and we returned to the clearing.

Last night we talked about the cutter, we dreamed about it, we worried about it. Never before had I seen Suvarrow's passage presenting such a wild and turbulent scene. Pratt has decided, in a like eventuality, to trust his life to the tree-house. Practically all the undergrowth between the clearing and the lagoon had been washed away. In the cockpit are the engine controls, the binnacle, and a thirty-six-inch hardwood wheel.

There are lots of people worse off than we, aren't there? We had missed being swept around the south point by a matter of yards and seconds! While sipping the Barbados rum I learned that John Pratt was a commercial artist.

CHAPTER TWENTY-SIX
THE HOUSE WITHOUT A KEY
(EARL DERR BIGGERS)

Not the kind of place where the mind rules. You know, you haven't read my palm since I was a child.

The older man thoughtfully tore it to bits and tossed them through the car window open beside him. In the lower section you'll find a battered strong box made of ohia wood and bound with copper.

The gangplank was taken up; clumsily the *President Tyler* began to draw away from the pier. It was in the eighties, as I told you, said the missionary. He went to the rail outside his stateroom. Just ask him if he recalls that day on Apiang Island in the eighties.

The next lad that makes a pass at me will find a different target. John Quincy gathered his wandering thoughts. How could I know that I was going up against the heavyweight champion in that attic? The girl moved swiftly toward the defenseless John Quincy. At first John

Quincy resented this, but gradually he began to feel that it didn't matter.

Was there anything in the world he wanted less? A few gulps, and you hit the ceiling of eternity. Not the kind of place where the mind rules.

A solitary light, like a star, gleamed in the distance.

I heard he had returned to Hawaii, and prospered. All wrong to come home so early, she cried. I aim to take particular care of you, sir. There's trouble waiting for us all, if we look far enough ahead.

The message appeared to be rather hastily scrawled. Jennison stood, the center of an admiring feminine group. Roger led the way up the grand staircase, then up a narrower flight. Well, that's that, she said finally, in a low voice. Happy days, continued the Dublin graduate, with a sigh.

The outer door of the kitchen stood open. I'll have a new glass put in that window to-morrow. Ever run for your life through crooked streets in the rowdy quarter of a strange town? After what seemed an age, Roger returned, bearing two lighted candles.

CHAPTER TWENTY-SEVEN
THE WHITE MONKEY
(JOHN GALSWORTHY)

Michael put his latchkey into the lock of his front door. Such things had been said to her before; but from Wilfrid it was serious. Isn't the Snooks Club meeting rather exciting?

The most distinguished Conversation ever held between the Dead. The furniture had come to a sudden standstill.

Fleur let her hand stay against his hot lips. Fleur's pen resumed its swift strokes, already becoming slightly illegible. A possibility; but suppose he wanted to play them something recent?

He came back to the hearth, and said: Ugly, isn't it? It was all frightfully amusing, frightfully necessary! She avoided unnecessary greetings or farewells. They might, she always felt, disapprove of women smoking in public halls. Would it bring him or would it put him off?

By Jove, that's a mot, or is it a bull; and are bulls mots or mots bulls? He'll read one specimen of every author and say: Oh! Reminded him that the state of love was a good stunt for poets.

And suddenly, dropping Ting-a-ling, she got up and began to walk about the room. Ting-a-ling was licking the copper floor. Fleur said coldly: You know very little; I AM fond of Michael. It also tells you how you may distribute copies of this Book if you want to. And suddenly, dropping Ting-a-ling, she got up and began to walk about the room.

Why, for instance, do we continually run ourselves down? A smile twisted his lips and eyebrows which resembled spinney's of dark pothooks.

There Hugo and the rest could see her taking her place in the English restoration movement. When those three came in she was sitting before a red lacquer tea-table, finishing a very good tea. She avoided unnecessary greetings or farewells.

In the present epoch, no Early Victorianism survives.

Consorting delicately with iconoclasm, Fleur never forgot that her feet were in two worlds at least.

The little dog's prominent round eyes gazed back; bright, black, very old. Desert said slowly: The moment I believe that, I shall go East.

In Fleur's involuntary smile was the whole secret of why her marriage had not been intolerable. The vice of our lot is, they say it pretty well, but they've nothing to say. The little dog's prominent round eyes gazed back; bright, black, very old. With circular movement of her squeezed hand, she said: Draw up.

CHAPTER TWENTY-EIGHT
SEVEN PILLARS OF WISDOM
(T. E. LAWRENCE)

He had cut across the hills by a difficult path to their great discomfort. We felt the stars were shifting and that we were steering wrong. Hardly, however, were we dear of the drifts beside the wells when there was an alarm.

Akaba bubbled immediately in an uproar about this circus beast. These tailings of valleys running into Sirhan were always rich in grazing. He had just bought a cream-coloured riding-camel of purest blood. We walked to our kneeling camels, and trotted after the company. His fashion of rising all at once from the food was of the central deserts.

They spoke eloquently: and sheet lightning in the west made gun-flashes for them. Pearl-diving in the gulf had made them like fishes in the water. We were up early, meaning to push the long way to Ammari by sunset. Though capable with camels, he was a shallow spirit, almost rabbit-mouthed, but proud.

Martin's summer, which passed like a remembered dream. I treated them exactly like the others in my bodyguard. Feisal told Abd el Kader to ride with Ali and myself, and said to me, I know he is mad.

He had just bought a cream-coloured riding-camel of purest blood. His young brother Adhub was taller and stronger, yet not above middle height. Mohammed, a villager at heart, fed too well. Zaal in October was not the Zaal of August.

He was an alert and hot-tempered lad of nineteen, with the petulance often accompanying curly hair. His large tents, with the women, had been sent away beyond reach of the Turkish aeroplanes. I felt his harsh beard brush my ear as he whispered to me windily, Beware of Abd el Kader.

Pearl-diving in the gulf had made them like fishes in the water.

Look at the dry stones for my bed-place, and for Tarfa's next it. They were the fighting men of the Serhan tribe on their way to swear allegiance to Feisal. Ali, furious with them, for their treacherous attack on us, threatened all sorts of pains.

My eyes were upon a notable red camel, perhaps a seven-year-old, under a Sirhani in the second line. Ahmed slipped off to get acquainted with her owner. Wood was ill, and lying on the platform of my old camp. It was peaceful, chilly, and very far from the fretting world.

Enough advantage for the time; we adjourned to eat with Mohammed el Dheilan. We walked to our kneeling camels, and trotted after the company. They had lost two men and a mare in the shooting on the railway in the night. Mounted men had been seen in the brushwood. Clouds of parching chalk dust arose, so that men's voices croaked.

CHAPTER TWENTY-NINE
IN GOOD KING CHARLES'S GOLDEN DAYS
(GEORGE BERNARD SHAW)

Our father lost his head by compromising with Protestants, Republicans, Levellers and Atheists. Well, what old Noll could do I can do; and so could you if you had the pluck. He keeps the biggest army in Europe; and he keeps you into the bargain. Well, that will seem very natural to the mob.

And you would send me back to France by the next ship, as you sent Barbara. It is a serious matter to lay hands on a royal personage. Both of them are rank Protestants and hardened soldiers, caring for nothing but fighting the French.

You still have love affairs: I have none.

Your brother is welcome here as long as you desire it. I am doing what I can to stop this Exclusion Bill and secure the crown for you when I die. I shall keep my eye on your Protestant bastard Monmouth.

Why is it that we always talk of my father's head and never of my great grandmother's? I have seen that book, and been astounded at the mental power displayed in every page of it.

But I can't do that without proper drapery: it's classical. You have done mischief enough for one morning. Meanwhile, however popular you may think yourself, you must go and be popular in Scotland.

I have too good reason to know that it is true. Will you get up, Jamie, and not sit on the floor grinning like a Jackanapes. I will take care that those who put me to it shall not die easy deaths.

Mr Newton is our host, Mr Kneller; and he is a very eminent philosopher. I hate blood and battles: I have seen too much of them to have any dreams of glory about them.

How vain is virtue which directs our ways
Through certain danger to uncertain praise!

I have not seen you practise it, Charles. All I need

is three or four different kinds of fish. I will fight my enemies if they put me to it. I have seen that book, and been astounded at the mental power displayed in every page of it.

If you had a pennorth of spunk in you you would burn the lot. I am not schooled and learned as you two princes are.

This painter has one kind of understanding: I have another.

CHAPTER THIRTY
THE SCANDAL OF FATHER BROWN
(G. K. CHESTERTON)

Baker seems to have taken them everywhere. We are the practical people; and that's why you're afraid of us. Father Brown patiently repeated the chemical formula he did not understand.

This is a special subject they call Applied Economics. I'm only a business man; and as a business man I think it's all bosh. And now they were resting from their labours and looking solemnly at the College gardens. And you've forgotten that there is one piece of external evidence that does really support history.

It's not our fault if nature made everything a scramble. I'm only a business man; and as a business man I think it's all bosh. Baker seems to have taken them everywhere. But now and then you do get a man who is a materialist, in the sense of a beast.

Let's begin with the first you mentioned. In many,

one might almost fancy, it would be almost automatic. You're trying to drag in mad insinuations about me, simply because you can't answer my question.

And now they were resting from their labours and looking solemnly at the College gardens. Isn't that evidence enough that there is a separate subject and may well be a separate Chair? For once he opened the conversation, by saying: No bodies washed ashore, I imagine. He kept it in his pocket till he wanted it; very likely he fired from his pocket.

Possibly you mean that little Muggleton murdered him himself. The only excuse was that they were foreigners.

You're trying to drag in mad insinuations about me, simply because you can't answer my question. By his own account, he bungled his case and let his patron be killed a few yards away.

After all, God made all the suns and stars to play Mulberry-Bush. Now we have all seen shabby actors, dirty actors, drunken actors, utterly disreputable actors.

CHAPTER THIRTY-ONE
THE HISTORY OF SPIRITUALISM
(ARTHUR CONAN DOYLE)

Compensation or retribution for good or evil deeds. They may be said to be roughly united upon seven central principles.

Fussey continued to suffer pain and exclaimed: Tab is wounded in the arm. Its appearance can be vouched for by sergeants and men of my section. Both the ladies have signed a document they sent me, affirming the accuracy of the above statement. But he stated afterwards that he had invented the incident.

The whole subject is freely discussed in the Constitutions. There are very many other prophecies which have been more or less successful. Both the beliefs therein expressed are articles of the Christian faith. He also referred to the new revelation as absolutely fatal to materialism.

A clergyman caught in a tavern was suspended.

Some weeks later his mother was tidying up the hearth in the sitting-room. He never gained a footing in our trenches. This exactly describes our own psychic experience, when séances are properly conducted.

Our SOS signal had been answered by our artillery. The cloud has gone from the end of his prospect. The early Christian graves present a strange contrast to those of the heathen which surround them.

I replied that I did not know any soldier near to me who had passed over. By the discovery of this mine the lives of a number of men were saved. A study of them reveals some curious facts.

There is no question of a supreme Bishop or Pope.

The whole subject is freely discussed in the Constitutions. In a number of cases dead soldiers have manifested themselves through psychic photography.

CHAPTER THIRTY-TWO
THE BETTY BOOK
(STEWART EDWARD WHITE)

It may mean merely obstructed tendencies or desires. It is stimulated in proportion to its response. It would be terrible were it not used for good.

Next, these advantages must be passed on; the spiritual circulation must flow unimpeded. Very uncomfortable, a kind of indigestion. Presently they showed Betty a picture illustrating this.

It works when we are not thinking of it if we will only think of it once in a while. There must be some definite relation you should have with your body, she exclaimed, puzzled. Weak prayer does not fulfill its part because it just calls down, instead of rising to meet. Only when this has been made habitual are we ready to proceed further.

The compensating treatment is in the roots of its life. But if you are sure-footed without being bountiful, you are merely ascetic.

Spirit dissolves the natural so curiously! It works just feebly, but after the manner of the whole big power. When the Invisibles first took up this subject they began it with a sidelight on the spiritual body. Unless it is alive it is not valuable even as a museum specimen.

Early in the game Betty was warned against trying to push ahead too far and too fast. At one period, though we continued to sit together, no spoken teaching was given.

Even mortification is submerged in eagerness to reconstruct and harmonize. So keep alternating your centers of consciousness frequently enough to get a proper proportion.

I can spread that way, comprehending, having contact, advancing. Stretch your arms and make your plan and take care they stay under your feet. There is something you can generate that both quickens your senses and subconsciously directs you. It seems like a failure that somebody is responsible for.

Something within you must rise continually to

meet the spiritual association. But if you start thinking about them much it livens: them up! Its an offering, a concentration of my life's experience returning to its source.

This is the region into which Betty has been led — the higher level of which she speaks. Reach out and touch it, and it stays with you — that's the secret. It is like a saturated solution of matter in spirit; I take up what I have strength for. But I can get through by means of this spiritual force.

That stratum must be lifted to raise the level of the whole. They say I have to look at it until I tell you about it.

Suppose one acknowledges all this. The spiritual body, we are assured, is indestructible.

CHAPTER THIRTY-THREE
MANY DIMENSIONS (CHARLES WILLIAMS)

What a time Giles is, showing Birlesmere the tombs in Westminster Abbey! Lord Birlesmere came back to the table and stood by Sir Giles. Look at the way Reginald adopted the Stone.

It took longer to satisfy the American than the scientist. Bruce Cumberland leaned across towards the Chief Justice. Then Sir Giles said suddenly: What about this foreign Power of yours? And really, Hajji, I don't know that I blame them.

But neither he nor anyone else of those concerned had any idea what to do next. No one, Lord Birlesmere exclaimed, is suggesting vivisection.

CHAPTER THIRTY-FOUR
THE PLUMED SERPENT (D. H. LAWRENCE)

There was silence, then the low hum of voices and the sound of laughter. There was silence, then the low hum of voices and the sound of laughter.

Repellent the strange heaviness, the sinking of the spirit into the earth, like dark water. Some, too shy to come right up, lingered on the nearest benches of the plaza. And when they could not breathe fire of the sun, they said: The sun is angry. A panic fear, a sense of devilment and horror thick in the night air. The man on the hill said: I am Quetzalcoatl, who breathed moisture on your dry mouths.

The Indians had come in from all the villages, and from far across the lake. The man at the drum lifted up his voice in a wild, blind song. The man on the hill said: I am Quetzalcoatl, who breathed moisture on your dry mouths. Bone triumphs in me, my heart is a dry gourd.

And Kate turned to the darkness of the lake. But she

heard the answer away back in her soul, like a far-off mocking-bird at night.

She did not know the face of the man whose fingers she held.

It was Saturday, and Sunday morning was market. It is I, the star, midway between the darkness and the rolling of the sun.

The clutching throb of gratification as the knife strikes in and the blood spurts out! It was like a darkly glowing, vivid nucleus of new life. When blue morning came they would cheer up. The whole village was in that state of curious, reptile apprehension which comes over dark people.

Beside him stood another man holding a banner that hung from a light rod. Kate could see nothing for the mass of men in big hats. It was she who lifted the motionless hand of the man in her own, shyly, with a sudden shy snatching. They were the irrepressible boot-blacks, who swarm like tiresome flies in a barefooted country.

But the police in most countries are never present save where there is no trouble. And perhaps it is this ponderous repudiation of the modern spirit which makes Mexico what it is.

CHAPTER THIRTY-FIVE
THE RED AND THE BLACK (STENDAHL)

The carriage is waiting, said the Marquis, as though to banish a vexatious thought. He had a narrow head with a large nose, and a curved face which he kept thrusting forward. Is it really possible, she meant nothing, nothing at all to my heart, only a few days ago. Politics in the middle of imaginative interests are like a pistol-shot in the middle of a concert.

It must be admitted that I am a very strange and very unfortunate creature. This evening you will have to look a little shabby. This evening you will have to look a little shabby. This was a flash of genius, cogent reasons followed in abundance. Mademoiselle de La Mole retorted proudly, who will dare to say to me that he has heard me?

Julien felt that it would have been more natural to call him the gentleman with the waistcoats. This is an error that stamps a superior person. Three seconds later the ladder was under the lime alley, and Mathilde's honour was saved.

His mirror shows the mire, and you blame the mirror!

Julien, overcome, was on the point of fetching back the ladder and mounting again to her room. Mathilde was enchanted; she saw in it a clear proof of her grand passion. At length the door opened, his name was called.

How lifeless they seem to me when compared with him, all copies of each other. The next thing was how to leave his little cane chair in a fashion that should not be too awkward.

She spoke to him against herself, she accused herself to him. It would be better, said Julien, to travel thirty leagues farther and avoid the direct route. Julien was greatly mortified, he was in the wrong. The luncheon bell just succeeded in waking him, he made his appearance in the dining-room. Julien saw that this was an allusion to something personal and highly offensive. One is esteemed in Paris for one's carriage, not for one's virtue.

The day passed like lightning; Julien was on the highest pinnacle of happiness. The noise is deafening without being emphatic. I wish to rid your petty self-esteem for ever of the ideas which it may have formed of me.

You shall have a formal letter of introduction. I am playing an undignified part here, he suddenly decided. The twofold remorse of her virtue and her pride made her, that morning, equally unhappy.

Her mother and one of the maids were aroused: immediately they called to her through the door. He was in a parlour hung in green velvet with broad stripes of gold. The carriage is waiting, said the Marquis, as though to banish a vexatious thought. He supplied himself with paper and wrote copiously.

Their true character was only now beginning to outline itself before his eyes. Ah, Sir, a novel is a mirror carried along a high road.

ABOUT THE "AUTHOR"

Jonathan Ball, PhD.

Author of stranger fiction.
Advocate of writing the wrong way.
Poet laureate of Hell.

www.JonathanBall.com